Social Media Marketing. Pinterest

Clear, Brief and Easy Strategy of Promotion

Table of Contents

Introduction

Chapter 1 what is Pinterest?

Chapter 2 The marketing Basics in Pinterest

Chapter 3 How to attract more followers in Pinterest

Enhanced social engagement

Optimizing your own webpage

Chapter 4 Pinterest for business

Chapter 5 10 Ways to earn Money from Pinterest

Conclusion

Introduction

I want to thank you and congratulate you for downloading the book, Pinterest.

This book contains proven steps and strategies on how to get profit from this social network.

The power and influence of Pinterest in shaping media trends and consumer choices is inarguable, but to allude to it as the new social media king may be a little inaccurate, or premature. But the consistently dismal number of male users on Pinterest does not seem to cause any serious dent on the social media site's overall performance. If anything, this even works to its advantage.

Consider the diversity of women on the site: Data from the Pew Research Center's Internet & American Life Project shows that as of February 2013, Pinterest is populated by well-to-do users, with about 20 percent of users having a total household income that exceeds $75,000, while only 10 percent of its users have a total household income under $30,000.

In addition, a more recent study by Forrester early this year revealed that majority of Pinterest users belong to Generations Z and Y, with each generation accounting to 27 percent of total users respectively. These are followed by members of Generation X running not too far behind at 19 percent, Baby Boomers at 14 percent, while members of the Golden Generation constitute the minority at six percent. The mix of users on Pinterest allows it to become the social media site with the highest conversion rate, far exceeding those by Facebook and Twitter. Companies and organizations that tap Pinterest as part of their marketing strategies have shown positive results as a result of traffic generated by their content pinned on the site.

Thanks again for downloading this book, I hope you enjoy it!

☐ **Copyright 2017 by Troy Baker - All rights reserved.**

This document is geared towards providing exact and reliable information in regards to the topic and issue covered. The publication is sold with the idea that the publisher is not required to render accounting, officially permitted, or otherwise, qualified services. If advice is necessary, legal or professional, a practiced individual in the profession should be ordered.

- From a Declaration of Principles which was accepted and approved equally by a Committee of the American Bar Association and a Committee of Publishers and Associations.

In no way is it legal to reproduce, duplicate, or transmit any part of this document in either electronic means or in printed format. Recording of this publication is strictly prohibited and any storage of this document is not allowed unless with written permission from the publisher. All rights reserved.

The information provided herein is stated to be truthful and consistent, in that any liability, in terms of inattention or otherwise, by any usage or abuse of any policies, processes, or directions contained within is the solitary and utter responsibility of the recipient reader. Under no circumstances will any legal responsibility or blame be held against the publisher for any reparation, damages, or monetary loss due to the information herein, either directly or indirectly.

Respective authors own all copyrights not held by the publisher.

The information herein is offered for informational purposes solely, and is universal as so. The presentation of the information is without contract or any type of guarantee assurance.

The trademarks that are used are without any consent, and the publication of the trademark is without permission or backing by the trademark owner. All trademarks and brands within this book are for clarifying purposes only and are the owned by the owners themselves, not affiliated with this document.

Chapter 1 what is Pinterest?

Pinterest is used by and large as a visual discovery tool. It's a bookmarking site that is both social and visual, which means users can share their media content (known as pins) to other users. These pins are generated on an average of two million each day. The images are either sourced from the World Wide Web or uploaded by the users themselves. They can later be organized according to themes in collections known as pin-boards.

One of the nice features of Pinterest is the ability to create pin-boards. Here, you organize your content based on a specific theme so that other users will not have to swim through random content. In making pin-boards, you have to be very strategic. Consider your target audience first: Who are they? What do they want? How can you make them look at your content?

Just as importantly, you need to pin regularly. The more you pin and re-pin images, the easier it will be for you to carve your niche on the site. Beware, however, from flooding the site by pinning content one after the other. You want to space out each pin evenly so that you don't end up annoying your followers with your relentless pinning.

At the same time, make sure to include snappy, SEO-ready captions to each media you pin, preferably with hashtags at the end. This will make it easier for users to find your content when they search using relevant keywords on the site's built-in search engine.

The same is true with the About Page. Each account on Pinterest comes with a section where you can introduce yourself or your organization. Make use of this section to advertise what your business is all about. Try to make this section brief by focusing on relevant keywords only. There is no need at all to write your company history in here.

Chapter 2 The marketing Basics in Pinterest

Pinterest is currently one of the most popular websites on the internet. This website is intended to help people create a database of links, images and videos of things that matter to them.

Though it is mostly dubbed as a crafter and DIY lovers' website, more and more people are joining Pinterest and reaping the benefits of creating and sharing a series of boards (collections of an idea) for inspiration, planning and organizing events or saving links, images, and videos on an online platform.

This free website is founded on the idea of a "personalized social media platform" that people can use and share for specific purposes. It allows people to save a link, image or video by "Pinning" it on a "Board". The board serves as an organizing tool, like a category for different topics that hold "Pins" that fall under the category.

Pinterest holds a large demography of users ranging from teenagers to adults, most of which are women. It is often compared to Google because it not only allows people to store pins and boards, but for research and discovering new websites and new ideas on the internet.

Bloggers, photographers, writer, illustrators and known personalities have been using Pinterest to share their interest and visual inspiration to their audience. Aside from its popularity, it also hosts different opportunities and advantages for businesses.

Because of this, it continues to attract businesses to open Pinterest accounts and use it to tap their audience and attract more visitors to their websites.

Pinterest is connected to different social media platforms including Twitter, Facebook and YouTube.

Users can automatically share their pins with just a click to all these social media sites, allowing their followers to view the pins even without a Pinterest account. The website also makes it easier for companies to create an online catalogue of products and items. Pinterest users and customers find it easier to shop, by simply browsing through the companies' boards and clicking on the image that directs them to the actual webpage. It also gives the company an opportunity to be discovered by Pinterest users by using tags and categories.

There are basic steps and strategies to use Pinterest in improving and curving the growth of a business upward. Here's a guideline of basic steps that websites can do to improve their business

Profiling
After creating a Pinterest account, make sure to feature the name of the business and include a link of the website. Add an interesting but informative paragraph about the business. This will be shown in the "About" section and will appear below the profile photo of the account. A good and interesting profile will help gain followers and entice other Pinterest users to check out the profile.

Connect to Social Media Sites
Connect the Pinterest account to various social networking sites including Facebook, Twitter and YouTube. Also add a "Pin" button to the website to help direct visitors to the Pinterest account. If the business has a blog, put up the Pinterest account on the blog.

Start Pinning
Create boards with creative and interesting names. Use this feature to pin products and images from the website. Add a caption and input tags. Use popular but related keywords to help other pinners discover the image posted on the Pinterest profile.

Connect with other Pinterest Users
Follow other Pinterest users. Comment on different pins and follow their board. It's also a good idea to join a "shared board". A shared board allows various Pinterest users to add their own Pins to the board as long as it fits the category of the board. This will help other people discover the pins of the website or business. It's also a great opportunity to start connecting with people and build a network of connections, people to collaborate with in the future.

Variety
Though it is important to showcase the products and images of the website, it is also important that the boards contain a variety of Pins from different websites. Pin interesting and captivating photos from different websites. Never pin an image directly found on Google Images. It is best to pin it from its original source. Consider pinning videos. Pinning videos is not very popular in Pinterest. If one wants to separate themselves from other pinners, try doing this.

Share on SNS
Aside from connecting the Pinterest account to social media accounts, use these SNS accounts to share the Pins on the Pinterest account. This will help increase traffic and followers.

Optimize
Optimize the website to automatically include a Pin button for each post and image. This will make it easier for other Pinterest users to share the image or link on their own profiles.

Watermark
Add a watermark or logo to the original images used in the website. This will ensure that no one takes

credit for the images when it is shared and pinned in various Pinterest accounts. However, when creating a watermark, make sure it doesn't block the entire photo. Position it in a way where it won't distract viewers.

RSS Feed

Every Pinterest account has its own RSS feed. You can use the RSS feed to advertise on various social networking sites so visitors can follow and be updated with new posts and pins.

Pinterest is a very effective marketing strategy when done properly. Take this opportunity to increase the audience and visitors of the website. Also, use this opportunity to start connecting with popular Pinterest users, including bloggers. Propose partnership or collaboration plans. This will help increase the customers of the business and increase the traffic on your website.

Aside from that, Pinterest makes it easier for other people to include the images and videos on the website in their own visual boards that they share with other people. It is also an engaging and creative way of cataloguing products and featuring campaigns and other advertisements.

The internet has changed the way business marketing is conducted. It has opened many new opportunities and possibilities to reach people from all over the world. It has provided a platform for customers from different countries to browse through websites and purchase from companies and businesses online.

Pinterest is just one of the platforms that has revolutionized and continues to redefine how marketing and advertising is done. Not only is it a friendly website and application, it also provides a cost-less avenue to market products, promote campaigns and advertisements; giving young businesses an opportunity to thrive and grow.

It has even surpassed other networking sites in terms of traffic and influence including LinkedIn, StumbleUpon and YouTube. While there are people who are busy using Pinterest for social and personal reasons, others are using it to connect and engage with customers in a visual, creative and appealing way.

Look into the possibilities of using Pinterest in business plans and campaigns and see how it affects the growth of a business or website.

Chapter 3 How to attract more followers in Pinterest

With over 70 million users and counting, Pinterest is fast emerging as one of the hottest social media networking sites today. Its focus on beautiful and compelling images makes it a standout from other equally popular sites. In fact, it now even serves as the go-to destination for online users wanting to learn more about wedding preparations, pick up new baking recipes, learn about exciting travel destinations, and in general cultivate a sense of visual inspiration.

There are a number of advantages and benefits on why creating a niche on Pinterest makes for a smart marketing strategy as far as you or your organization is concerned.

For starters, there's money to be made on Pinterest. Unlike Facebook or Twitter where the most you can do is create hype for your brand, on Pinterest you can reasonably expect to generate leads and actual sales. Did you know, for example, that half of those who have seen product recommendations on Pinterest eventually end up availing them?

One of the biggest mistakes many new Pinterest users commit, however, is the tendency to focus heavily on acquiring followers without first checking their own content. Whether you like it or not, the quality of your pins will by and large determine either the success or failure of your managed account.

Pinterest allows you to create comprehensive visual bookmarks of webpages that can be shared socially. Emphasis should be duly placed on the word "visual." In a site with millions of gorgeous images, the key challenge lies in how to make your original content stand out.

Content is king

The answer is fairly simple: create quality content. Do not pin blurry, out of focus, pixelated, poorly lit, or overly saturated photos. Strive to produce images that tell a story or convey a sense of drama.

On average, a pin on Pinterest gets re-pinned at least 10 times. So in general, the sharper and prettier the image, the better chances of being shared and creating a buzz to your account. But pinning gorgeous images on your account is not enough. More importantly, you have to write effective and concise captions that are specific and SEO-rich.

You can also write hashtags at the end of your captions. Remember, an integral aspect of increasing the number of your followers is having an easy accessibility of your content. You can't have followers if you have obscure and hard to find pins.

At the same time, be mindful of the frequency with your content. Try to update your pin-boards on a regular basis, but make sure to even out the intervals between each post. After all, you do not want to flood others with your content.

Note that pinning regularly makes your account exciting and provides your followers something to look forward to. If you do not pin on a regular basis, you miss out on two things:

First, other Pinterest users will be turned off by your inactivity. Second, you would lose out on the opportunities for leads and sales that could have otherwise been generated by new and updated pins.

A very crucial aspect of getting more followers is placing a heavy emphasis on the social nature of Pinterest. So check out accounts similar to yours and follow them. Find out the most popular users and engage with them either by leaving comments on their pins or mentioning them on your posts.

Enhanced social engagement

Acknowledge the other users who follow you or take time to leave comments on your account. Try to respond to their comments if you can in order to build greater social engagement within your pin boards.

In creating these pin-boards, you should always know your audience. You should know their wants, needs, and their preferences so it will be much easier to create a customized experience for them.

The more dynamic your account, the better it is. To help you identify the kind of pins that will generate the most buzz or interest, have a social media calendar ready. Identify the holidays, occasions, or events that call for specific posts.

Christmas, Valentine's Day, Mothers' and Fathers' Days, end of school, the start of spring break, Fourth of July, Thanksgiving Day, and other momentous days signify an opportunity to get in touch with certain audiences. This targeted approach in pinning content will certainly maximize the exposure of your account and increase the chances of attracting new followers.

A sure way to create buzz, however, is by sponsoring contests and promotions. Guaranteeing exciting prizes always makes for a good marketing strategy as long as your contests are entertaining and easy to participate in. Require all contestants to follow your account. For instance, offering a chance to win a prizes is an easy and relatively hassle-free way of collecting more followers to your account. Just be sure to follow through with the promise to avoid negative backlash.

Optimizing your own webpage

Outside of Pinterest, there are also a handful of things you can do to make others be familiar with your account and become eventual followers themselves. One of the things you can do is insert the Pinterest button on your website or blog. Place this button at the end of each article or right next to an image on your webpage to make it easier for your web visitors to re-pin your content.

You can also create a Pinterest widget and place it on a prominent part of your page. This widget is supposed to show a glimpse of your pins and pin boards in order to entice others to go check your account.

And finally, do not forget to link your Pinterest account with your other social media networks. This is to make managing your accounts more efficient, seamless, and integrative. Link your Pinterest account, for example, with Facebook or Twitter to let others know your new pins.

At the same time, you can also try to pin the images on your Instagram or Facebook account, or create special pin boards based on the content from your other social media feeds. The possibilities are endless. You just need to be imaginative, creative, and strategic.

In sum, Pinterest serves as a great marketing tool for people or organizations that want to boost their company profile, enhance traffic to their content, or improve their bottom line.

Take note, however, that similar to the case of Facebook and Twitter, having more followers isn't necessarily better, especially when a huge bulk of your followers do not have a stake in your organization's overall goals and objectives. So in trying to increase your followers on your Pinterest account, it is important that you end up attracting the kind of crowd that you want, the kind that will promote greater customer engagement and enhance the performance of the products or services you offer.

You can do this by being strategic and by spending a fair amount of time producing quality content, interacting with your followers, and optimizing your own blog or website. The strategies listed above should serve as effective measures to kick start your journey to eventual success on Pinterest.

Chapter 4 Pinterest for business

It is common for people to use the Internet to search for all kinds of information. While a diverse amount of data can be found in an instant, keeping all those searched information organized and accessible can often be difficult and overwhelming.

Pinterest is now considered an important aspect of most B2B or B2C social media marketing strategies. It is practically a database of things that people would like to have or find interesting, which may be a valuable piece of information to marketers and advertisers.

While Google analyzes numbers to figure out what is significant, Pinterest users already define and emphasize what is relevant for a given topic.

As the third most popular social networking website in the world, Pinterest can be a great tool for ecommerce stores to increase their website traffic and boost sales and finance. From the traffic generated by Pinterest, shoppers are 10 percent more likely to make a purchase compared to those who arrive from other social sites.

In fact, over twenty percent of the Pinterest users that were surveyed said they bought an item from the actual store after pinning, re-pinning, or liking it.

To best optimize Pinterest for businesses, here are some suggestions:

Complete and enhance your company or business profile. Make sure that the Pinterest profile features the following:

A significant image that represents your business and preferably one that matches your other social networks (Twitter, Facebook Page, etc.) for easier recognition by your target audience.

Include a short profile of the business that briefly explains your identity and encourage people to learn more about you. This should be consistent as well with your profile on your other social networks or website.

Include your verified website so that your Pinterest profile visitors can instantly refer or be linked to your official website.

Include a clickable link to your Twitter and Facebook accounts as well.

Create boards on your Pinterest account that relate to keywords for which you would like to rank on google. For example, a caterer may want to create boards for wedding parties, family reunions, events and other types of services. Apart from the SEO factor, your visitors can get a quick insight into what your business is about and what you have to offer.

Pin images and videos based on your target audience's interests and behavior. In content marketing, the goal is to create content that your target audience and potential customers will be drawn to.

Monitor the pinning activity from your website. Just like how you acknowledge the people who re-tweet you on twitter or share content from your Facebook

Page, you may also want to interact with those who have pinned images directly from your website.

Chapter 5   10 Ways to earn Money from Pinterest

1. Personal Artwork

Artists have long relied upon galleries to display the work they wish to share with the world. Unfortunately, not every artist can obtain a gallery showing. Even when they do, the customer base is limited to those who enter the gallery with the intention of spending. Pinterest gives artists of all types a platform for sharing their artwork with interested potential buyers.

The question of copyright does rear its head where original artwork is concerned. As an artist, you may dislike the notion of his or her art being shared without their permission. Unfortunately, this keeps many artists from taking advantage of a Pinterest storefront to display their art. Most artists find that having their artwork shared with the world is a positive experience regardless of how it is shared. You will see much higher profits from sharing your artwork on Pinterest than from simply waiting for someone to find you.

2. Consignment

Shoppers who wish to save big bucks on everything from clothing to large appliances visit consignment shops. These spots allow consumers to purchase gently used items at remarkable discounts. In recent years, consignment events have drawn large crowds who wish to view multiple types of products at once. By placing consignment items online, you offer your customers one more way to save. You can also avoid the fees that are charged by online auction sites or other third party web presences.

The easiest way to advertise consignment items on Pinterest is to group your items into specific boards. Pinterest users love unique products, handmade items, and antiques. They want to find those things that either make their lives easier or decorate their homes in a stylish way. One-of-a-kind clothing items are also welcome on Pinterest boards. Vintage toys are also a fun idea.

A mistake that is made by some Pinterest users with consignment storefronts is placing each and every item on Pinterest. Those products that are not unique or original in some way only take up space on Pinterest boards, annoying users who then will disregard your posts as spam. Be sure to stay present on Pinterest, but only with those images that will intrigue users enough to click through to your main site. From that point, they can explore the rest of the products that you have available.

3. Direct Sales

Direct Sales has long offered a way to try new products and introduce them to friends while making money. The time-tested method of selling wares like handbags, kitchen items, and candles is to ask individuals you know to host product parties in their home. They then invite their friends and acquaintances to socialize and shop.

In recent years, companies like Pampered Chef and 31 have embraced the online culture to allow their sales consultants to employ their own websites in order to sell to a wider customer base. They encourage consultants to set up product sites, blogs, and social media pages, including Pinterest.

4. Automobiles

Sites like eBay and Craigslist have become surprisingly effective tools for selling used vehicles. By creating honest profiles with significant detail and scores of pictures, sellers can get fair prices for their automobiles and buyers can feel confident in their purchases. Motivated buyers have no issue with traveling long distances, sometimes across state lines, for great deals on used cars.

Though most dealerships have websites these days, more and more customers avoid them so that they may bypass higher prices and haggling. Alternatively, purchasing from small businesses or individuals is much more attractive to those who wish to pay a lower price for a quality item.

5. Latest Trends

Watch the trends that take the online world by storm and you can capitalize on the new sensation in an easy and enjoyable way. The current culture might be obsessed with bacon, early 20th century mustaches, or zombies. Find a way to incorporate these images on t-shirts, aprons, even packets of gum and you can make money and have fun.

One of the main benefits in focusing on trends is that you can always have a rotating stock. Housing a limited supply of items means that you will be unlikely to have tired products left on the shelves while you look for the next big thing. You can also virtually guarantee that you will stay on the cutting edge of society's likes and dislikes by always keeping in touch with the ever-fluctuating culture.

6. Gift Baskets

Gift baskets are ideal for literally every occasion. The baskets can be small enough to hold only one or two items or as large as a trunk for a vast array of objects. You can offer pre-made gift baskets or give your customers the chance to create their own. The options are limitless.

Gift baskets are ideal for baby showers, wedding showers, and birthdays. However, they also work well for anniversaries, as bon voyage presents, for housewarmings, and to celebrate graduations. The secret to creating gift baskets for these occasions and any others that may come along is to stock your shelves with as wide of a variety of containers and objects as your budget will allow.

7. Food Items

Food is a powerful motivator for all Pinterest users. They love to look at pictures, search for recipes, and salivate over the delicious items that are presented to them with each new pin. A storefront that specializes in shippable delicacies can be one of the most lucrative choices of all.

Selling food through the internet can sometimes be problematic, but it can be done. Be certain that your food is prepared with the utmost care regarding safety and hygiene. Shipping food must be done with great care as well. You will need to thoroughly research the best way to ship each item you create. For instance, some items might need to be shipped via overnight delivery for freshness. Frozen items might require dry ice. You will also need to make sure that you charge appropriately but not unreasonably.

8. Personal Training

Almost every Pinterest user has a board that is devoted to exercise. Nearly everyone wants to lose a few pounds or tone a particular body part. Personal Trainers can advertise their services on Pinterest by sharing a few effective moves. The best are pinned again and again, creating repeat advertising for your business.

9. Photography

Photography has changed greatly in recent years. Thanks to high-powered, easy-to-use cameras, even an average user can take decent photographs. In addition, services like Instagram allow everyday photographers to become artists in their own right. Professional photographers must now compete with casual users in a way that they never have before.

Still, there is high demand for photographers who display their skill on their Pinterest boards.

To get the most out of Pinterest, focus on your preferred subject while keeping others in mind. Most photographers have a niche, like wedding photography, newborn photography, or portraits. You should highlight this niche, but also have a portfolio available that shows your talents in other areas. You should also display some flexibility. Let it be known how far you are willing to travel for your art. Have a wide variety of packages from which your customers can choose.

10. Vacation Planning

Travel agencies may not be in as high demand as they were before the likes of Travelocity and Expedia.com. Still, entire careers are based around individual vacation planning. Practically every urban area in the country is home to at least one individual who makes a living from planning others' trips to Disney World alone. Use your personal vacation planning skills to help others learn how to budget their time and money. Help them to find the best vacation for their needs. Get them the best prices on hotels, transportation, entertainment, and food.

Pinning vacation photos is the best way to link back to your site. However, you can provide great information on the photographs themselves. For instance, pin a picture of Roatan, Honduras and caption it with a few words about the fabulous, low cost resort area and your number. You might be surprised at the number of calls you receive.

Conclusion

Thank you again for downloading this book!

Given the right social media strategy and implementation, Pinterest may actually offer any business more referral traffic than twitter, and perhaps generate more leads than LinkedIn, Google + and YouTube combined.

It may even have the power to convert more fans into paying customers who will easily share your content with their friends

www.ingramcontent.com/pod-product-compliance
Lightning Source LLC
Chambersburg PA
CBHW061234180526
45170CB00003B/1288